D1602491

DO NOT REMOVE
CARDS FROM POCKET

THE STATIC ELEMENT

THE
STATIC
ELEMENT

Selected Poems of

NATAN ZACH

Translated by

PETER EVERWINE

and

SHULAMIT YASNY-STARKMAN

Atheneum 1982 *New York*

Some of these translations, in earlier versions, first appeared
in *Keeping the Night*, Atheneum, and *Voices Within the Ark*, ed.
Howard Schwartz and Anthony Rudolf, Avon.
"No," "The Problem," "Nothing to Shout About," and
"To Rise from Ashes" originally appeared in *Grand Street*.

LIBRARY OF CONGRESS CATALOGING IN PUBLICATION DATA

Zach, Nathan.
The static element.

1. Zach, Nathan—Translations, English. I. Everwine,
Peter. II. Yasny-Starkman, Shulamit. III. Title.
PJ5054.S18A23   1982   892.4'16   82–71257
ISBN 0–689–11318–8
ISBN 0–689–11319–6 (pbk.)

Composed and printed by Heritage Printers, Inc., Charlotte, North Carolina
Bound by The Delmar Company, Charlotte, North Carolina
Designed by Mary Cregan
First Edition

CONTENTS

BIOGRAPHICAL NOTE

Born in Berlin in 1930, Natan Zach (variously transliterated as Sach or Zakh) immigrated with his family to Israel in 1935. One of Israel's most important poets, as well as a writer of influential critical essays, he has been described by Shimon Sandbank as "the most articulate and insistent spokesman" of the modernist movement in Hebrew poetry.

Zach began to write as a student at the Hebrew University of Jerusalem. Following the publication of *First Poems* (SHIRIM RISHONIM, 1955) and *Various Poems* (SHIRIM SHONIM, 1960), he was closely associated with Israeli theater until 1967, first as Repertory Director for the Trade Unions' OHEL theater and later as advisor to the Chambre Theater in Tel-Aviv. He has translated plays by Brecht, Dürrenmatt, Frisch, Strindberg, and others. During this period he also published his third volume of poems, *All the Milk and the Honey* (KOL HE'KHALAV VE'HADVASH, 1964), and a collection of poems of travel in Italy, *A Dream Instead* (BIMKOM KHALOM, 1966). With the Palestinian poet Rashed Hussein he co-translated *Palms and Dates* (DEKALIM U'TEMARIM, 1967), a collection of Palestinian Arab folk-songs.

After 1968 Zach settled in Britain where he completed a doctorate from the University of Essex and worked as the London news editor for the Jewish Telegraphic Agency. He returned to Israel in 1979 and presently teaches at Haifa University.

His most recent collection is *North-Easterly* (TSEPHONIT MIZRAKHIT, 1979). In 1981 he received the Bialik Prize, Israel's most distinguished literary award.

PREFACE

The poems of Natan Zach share something of the astringent style that has become familiar in the distressed literature of post-war modernism. Having been subjected to extraordinary historical pressures, they are guarded in tone, oblique, frequently satiric and pointed with wit, deliberately reductive. "It's the salt in me that talks," Zach says in one of his poems, a distillation clearly antidotal to the overtly national and ideological poetry that, in his words, had satisfied "a previous generation's thirst for grand certainties." There are few certainties, grand or otherwise, to hold fast to in his work. To follow the movement of a Zach poem is to follow a nervous and analytical intelligence that refuses to be taken in by conventions of sentiment or piety. A tenacious ironist, deeply aware of human isolation and the elaborate illusions we construct as our refuges (the refuge of poetry included), his characteristic attitude is "Be careful . . . Don't expect." His reticence becomes a way of holding things in check, an integrity that is both a literary position and a personal response to experience.

Zach is a difficult poet to translate. He can be the sparest and most colloquial of poets, but he also exploits fully the unique character of Hebrew—that ancient language "torn from its sleep in the Bible" (Yehuda Amichai) and revived to the demands of a changed world. Like other Israeli poets, he moves easily among biblical and liturgical referents, but he is innovative in the way he rapidly juxtaposes various linguistic levels. Biblical phrase is set against flat banality; hyperbole is set against laconic understatement or the lingo of the streets. Thus he exploits language and also subjects it to implicit criticism, attacking fashionability and cant. Essentially a dramatic poet, his conversational rhythms are equally complex in counterpoint, and he often uses rhyme—especially internal rhyme—as a device to cancel or counterbalance statements of excessive intensity or pomposity. The effect is frequently one of restless improvisation and tension, and it is a music and a texture of meaning that a translator can only attempt to approximate. A flat literal version is certain to drain him of major effects.

A case in point: I once showed to Zach an early version of "Failure," feeling quite smug in having captured—or so I believed—a rather plaintive tone in a poem that spoke quietly of the persistence of desire and its inevitable failure. Zach was horrified. I had "softened" his poem considerably, accurately catching its literal meaning but failing to consider the function of his abrupt rhymes and shifts in idiom. I had lost the proper distancing of his irony. My version spoke of pathos; his poem articulated a judgement. So much for tender-mindedness.

This difficulty is somewhat diminished in Zach's most recent work. In what seems to be an effort to accomodate a broader range of materials and "to speak to the moment, like a journalist," he has loosened his forms considerably. As he says in "The Problem," the poet must find a form that is

> like a diamond, but also like an ample bed
> where a man can stretch without
> knocking his head against a wall,
> and like a taut string
> with no corners to catch dust.

These paradoxical demands seem characteristic of the tensions in Zach's work. Never a comfortable poet, he reminds us that a poem is an ambiguous system of insights, a "static element" addressed to the immediacy of the moment and engaged in the daily coming and going of our perplexed lives. Shaped by the artificer's traditional cunning, it is like an intricately fashioned net in which the rare and the redeemable may yet be surprised, "here and there,/blossoming." It is not a poetry of optimism or easy affirmation, but at times there rises a guarded belief that

> There is something in promises—
> remote, a secret wrapped in desires
> no one can unravel—

> the wadi winding its way,
> the city that rose from salt,
> the strange end of Job:
> forms of things to come.
>   (*"A Gust of Warm Wind"*)

A guarded belief, not a cause for celebration. As Zach says,

> A starry night?
> No. Not yet.
> (*"On the Impossibility of the Unromantic Condition"*)

*

Despite Zach's stature as a poet and his importance to the development of Hebrew poetry, he is virtually unknown to an English-speaking audience. A slim pamphlet of his poems, translated by the poet Jon Silkin, appeared in England under the title *Against Parting* (October House, 1967), but this has not been easily available. What thus began as my own effort to read and understand his work has evolved over the years into this present collection.

The translations that follow are drawn from Zach's published volumes to date, with the exception of his Italian travel poems. The order of poems in each section is my own. A number of poems I wanted to include had to be abandoned; my English was not adequate to their demands.

As for the method of translation: I worked from literal cribs, glosses, and notes prepared by Shulamit Yasny-Starkman, a native Israeli. Each version was then subjected to critical discussion and subsequent revisions. The final result, therefore, has been a true collaboration, although the responsibility for any deficiencies must be mine alone. I am aware that this method leaves much to be desired. My purpose here is not to defend it but simply to acknowledge it. Within the limits of my understanding and ability, my intention was to provide a clear, immediate sense of Zach's rigorous and unique poetry.

I am indebted to a number of friends who read versions of the manuscript and gave me the benefit of their critical insights, especially to Bill Broder, Philip Levine, and Robert Mezey.

I am especially grateful to Natan Zach for his hospitality, his valuable comments, and his cooperation throughout this project. More than this, his support carried me through those times when I believed that no man in his right mind would undertake the task of translation.

Finally, I am pleased to acknowledge a long-standing debt of gratitude to Harry Ford.

Peter Everwine

I

from EARLY POEMS: 1955

Be careful. Open your life
only to the wind that has touched distance.
Suffer the absent. Speak up
only in the nights of solitude. Know the day,
the fixed season, the moment,
and don't beg. Pay attention to what is still. Learn to bless
the shadow just beneath the skin. Don't
hide in words. Sit with the counsel of worms,
the wisdom of the maggot. Don't expect.

They unloaded the gold of Ophir
in the harbor.
A band was playing
beyond the shutters.
And I knew it was forbidden.
Forbidden.
In fifteen years,
or thirty,
or forty-five—
perhaps only then
I'll lie, like this,
in a dark room,
undressed,
dead quiet,
when they unload the gold.

*Ophir: biblical land of gold.

The small, stifling room follows
ten steep, iron steps, followed by
a sharp, hot splinter
of moon. And in between,
sticky light as if smeared on walls
by the *hamsin**, too listless even to stir
the laundry hanging from the tenements.

The echo of each movement returns you
to yourself—vague silhouette—as to a lullaby.
You remember and accept again
the body on the chair, head leaning
on the table, a finger
in the dust of darkness.

This is the breathing space between one solitude
and another, an oppressive reading
in a book that recedes from you—from this
momentary rest between demand
and slackness—moving out
into the open night

that knows you instantly by your hesitations.

hamsin: a hot, dry and oppressive wind of the Middle East.

Even stones in the wall will cry out—
if they haven't cried out by now.
A city will break into song—
if it hasn't sung by now.
A tourist in the hotel. A pregnant woman.
A field-grade officer.

Wind will go down to the sea—
if it hasn't gone down by now.
A supple body will stir the blood.
A woman from yesterday. A map of sand.
One person to another.

The landscape loses its name—
if it hasn't been lost by now.
The street dust turns again
into drifting sand.
A hundred dollar bill. A painted door.
Alone.

Also a little fraud in loneliness
Also a little bribery in solitude
Also a little blackmail in distress
Also a little theft in keeping removed

There's a deep root that grows nothing
There's a secret gall that grows sweet

II

from VARIOUS POEMS: 1960

II

When God first said Let there be light
He meant it would not be dark for Him.
In that moment He didn't think about the sky,
but the trees already were filling with water,
the birds receiving air and body.
Then the first wind touched God's eyes
and He saw it in all His glory
and thought It is good. He didn't think then
about people, people in their multitude,
but they already were standing apart from the fig leaves,
unraveling in their hearts
a scheme about pain.
When God first thought of night
He didn't think about sleep.
So be it, God said, I will be happy.
But they were multitudes.

I've had enough! said the old man
and carefully shut the gate
behind him.

The boy, barely visible,
was growing smaller
at the end of the alley.

Everything goes! said the old man.
Pain has its way in the end.
He turned and slept then.

And only one little finger,
dreaming of the world beyond the door,
whispered to itself—I want more!

But the cockroach spat
and said in its bitter tongue
—That's that.

Nothing comes.
The night wind stirs its darkness
like night wind stirring its darkness.
Nothing comes.

Nothing comes.
The door that was closed and opened
opened and closed.
Nothing comes.

Nothing comes.
Legs crossed, lamp on the table,
a shadow and an undershirt.
The one who entered is the one who left.
Nothing comes.

Not at night, no, anyway, tomorrow,
she will not come today, today it's cold,

no, if at all, not in the dark, alone,
shadow on a wall, hand on heart, not an agitated heart,

not in fear, no, if at all, not in rain,
not like a spear, not footsteps in the rain, not a net

of water, not a black sky, not a cloud,
not a small cloud, not now, under a green tree,

not in the street, if at all, not at the gates of the house,
not by hand, not slowly, not in the heat, under an olive tree,

not today, not from necessity, not hard,
not in sunlight, not like a sword.

Here they come, please look!
By the time you get here, they've gone, she said.
In the garden the worm bit deeper
into the flesh of the fruit.
It hurts! said the dog to its master.
The master ignored it. Master,
you can't imagine how it hurts.

It's only a coffin with something in it.
Nothing is left of the face.
Children ran off with the parts.

Are you searching for a path in the sea?
Do you expect to see him
awake or asleep?

As for me, I don't know.
In the eyes of others I seem a deceiver.
But as for me, I don't know.

No, I'm not searching for a path in the sea.
And yes, I've been here, also I've been there.
In my opinion, the table should be moved.

The woman said she didn't like words.
I don't pass a thing on to others.
In my opinion, things aren't reliable.

Yes, walk with me in my coming and going.
The streets are quiet, the alleys fragrant.
You may come with me.
You may also wait.
Now, alone. Later, with the music.

From year to year it grows more refined,
it will be so very refined in the end—
she said, speaking of it.

But sometimes I feel I'm drowning in time,
I feel I've been drowning a long time—
he said.

It's because you're sinking, she said.
You know, it's all because you're sinking.

I don't know. Sometimes I think my strength has fled.
Refined, you know, is another word for negative.

I know and I applaud you for your discoveries.
I applaud you for your charming subtleties.
You leave nothing behind you.

But that's exactly my anxiety!
But that's exactly what will be said of me!
But that's exactly what I feel!

You're wrong again: you feel good, and goodness surrounds you.
Goodness, in fact, is really all around you.
Be patient, it will show its face to you.
No sooner done, it will surely embrace you.
A little time goes by, then it must kiss you.
You know how one thing leads to another.

When God in the Bible wants to promise
He points to stars. Abraham strolls
from his tent at night
and sees lovers. As sand on the sea shore,
the Lord says. And man believes,
even though he understands that to say
as sand is merely a way
of speaking.
And from that time on,
sand and stars have been intertwined in
man's net of images. But perhaps
we shouldn't speak here of man.
He wasn't mentioned there and then—

and yet it is said explicitly *as sand*,
from which we might infer
the capacity for enduring. On the other hand,
it's possible to believe
that everything is then set free
and there are no more—explicitly
no more—boundaries.

As sand on the sea shore. But then, water
is never mentioned. God does, however,
speak of seed. Which only goes to show
the ways of heaven
and possibly, those of nature.

I've never understood Samson's hair:
that power concealed in it, his hermetic secrecy,
the interdiction—not to be defied—
never to speak of it,
and the terrible anxiety
of being shorn, the horror each time
Delilah slips her fingers through his locks.

On the other hand
I understand quite well the hair of Absalom.
Obviously it's beautiful, like the noon-day sun,
like a red moon of vengeance,
sweeter than the many fragrances of women.
Ahithophel, sly and cunning, has to look away

when he beholds the reason for David's love.
This is the most marvelous hair in the kingdom—
which, as you can see,
explains the outbreak of each new rebellion
and later, that business of the tree.*

*In the battle of Ephraim's wood, Absalom's head is caught up in the boughs
of an oak as he rides beneath it. Helpless, he is then killed by Joab.

A boy hammers on a girl's door.
The girl doesn't open it.
The boy's head is spinning.
The girl's head is spinning.
Thousands of angels escort the sun on its way,
flying in that unique formation peculiar to angels.
Have you ever loved me? he asks.
I love you, she answers, in a halting voice.

A boy hammers on a girl's door.
The girl doesn't open it.
I love you, answers the girl,
and for the first time the boy discovers
in himself true generosity.

The angels get tired. Everything made of earth
gets tired. The boy does not get tired.
A boy hammers on a girl's door.
Be astonished, O ye heavens and earth! Who knows
why a boy discovers the meaning of true generosity?

Like the mountain, says the mother. Like the mountain,
says the child, learning by rote his mother's old saw.
Like the mountain, says the boy, putting two and two together.

Who understands why the boy is hammering on the girl's
door? Who knows why the girl doesn't
open it?

I love you, whispers the girl. I love you,
repeat the stars, the pets in the house.
I love you, whispers the Angel of Death
in his pure, geometric voice.
A boy hammers on a girl's door.
How does it happen that precisely now
he learns the true meaning of generosity?

Seven times the wolf said to the lamb,
Beware! On the eighth he devoured it.

What brought me to want
whatever it is the heart wants?

Or led me to believe I might divide
water from water

that cannot be divided
and only in the sky

is altered to air?
Meanwhile

only the heart is still there, wishful
as ever,

and whatever was not fished up
on its hook.

To be the master of your house, to wrestle
against winds, to sit beneath the fig tree,

to be watchful of the foxes that spoil
the vines, to read in the book of dust,

to know the festivals of light cast down
at your feet, to be wary of stolen water as of fire,

to touch each object twice, to sit a long time
and not look up at the clouds

passing overhead at night
on their way to the sea.

I've grown away from my grandfather
while playing music. No longer do I wait
for his utterance under the piano
or listen for my name when he sings.
It seemed to me I was getting closer
and yet I'm farther.
It seemed to me he forgot,
and it is I who have forgotten.

Sometimes I asked the pilots to bring me
my iron ration straight to the shelter where I hid.
I don't believe in idols;
nonetheless, I wasn't answered. The war
passed over my head. They didn't know the way,
there wasn't an air bridge, they said.
I don't smoke American cigarettes, not even
before sleep. I don't go up in planes.
I'm not that naive.

He disappeared in the fog. They say his fuel
ran out. No point in making a fuss
over what's done with. Provided, of course,
the family doesn't inquire.
The fatigue of matter—that's reason enough.
In cities grown weary of matter
laments of napthaline drift in colored darkness
as in an alchemic liquid from the Middle Ages.
The meticulous gentleman of my own age
is counting worn coins—
worthless, without future,
and dug up, layer by layer—
late dust witnessed by a dimmed, final vision.

Hands trembling, the antiquary unfurls
the genealogical scroll, canceled long ago.
In an untheatrical light of the sun
his hairy hands seem immense. Monsters, by comparison,
are microbes magnified by water. Mountains
are only places to come down from. Airplanes are bees
that stopped buzzing. They gather bombs, not honey,
with hands, not wings, hazarding dust and sleep.
Deceit lights its fires on the hills to signal
one more conclusion. And balding scoundrels
huddle together in debate,
pointing to maps that even yesterday
had nothing to hide beneath the sand.

On your forehead now
the everlasting flower.
Invisible worms
are nourished at your cheeks.
On maneuvers your name
is seldom mentioned. Your flesh
is like a sieve: you leave
and enter as you wish. But your hand,
like a watch that marks the earth's time,
still troubles my hours.
Before you came I had believed it necessary
to hurry to my task.

I don't know what you think of children these days.
It's even difficult to picture
your face when I'm afraid.
It seems that events
have already moved on,
as to a late reel of film, beyond recall.
But in the desert they still worship you
in soldiers' boots. The bramble
remembers the sound of your commands
and bows.

Sergeant Weiss, I don't know how much time will pass
before I suddenly remember you,
restless again.
Perhaps you were right. You built your house
where you can't be reached except by cold, heat, hunger,
desire perhaps. Water will not well around your eyes,
the oleander will not sing in your tongue.
Your mother is dead, Sergeant Weiss.
You will not be a child again.

In this eternal parody of men's fates
war takes one of the leading parts.
Styled by the inarticulate, it never knows
its image: it engulfs you like a sea
that bores through the swimmer's flesh and rushes on—
to death, victory—headlong,
heedless of all but motion.
Your madness is one possibility,
not the worst. You, at least, create a condition
we can't appeal.

But at the heart of these illusions that vanish
and leave nothing behind to show
they existed, I sometimes see
your amazed eyes, like oases
that aren't mine. We who were unable, all these years,
to shape war into something we can grasp
remember you as a densely written page—illegible,
perhaps, but correct, setting down the days that passed
and were not fulfilled.

1

How the days passed! Who would have thought
they pass like this. How time passes, and the sky,
even the wind!

The wind whirled once in the tree, despising our memories.
You who were once mine
do not belong now
even to the stars.

2

Under the fallen leaves autumn lay waiting
for its time, secret as the locust.
Slowly, so very slowly, the body's rain falls,
the terrifying hair withers.

A piece of driftwood on the shore
draws comfort from the wind.

Fish slide away from the surface
in a heavy murmur. Young forever,
their eyes are petrified water.

The place they will set aside for us
one day in another place
is preparing itself:
the earth never tires of being opened.

Already I hear the riders galloping
on the plain. Mother! the boy cried, I can see
their iron hooves! Hush, said the mother. Hush,
child I bore, child I gave the world,
you see nothing.

When will strange diamonds blossom from the
coal of my eyes? When will I see you again
and hold you, and my lips
whisper of love?

I don't know. To be exact: I do not know.
What I had, I tried to give. Such matters
are long and weary. This isn't the place to speak of them.
They didn't change the world.
It's the salt in me that talks.

When the last riders disappear over the horizon
and even the dust of their horses no longer rises
I'll know it is time to lock the gate.
The spent day will look at its hands and be content.
For me the hour will be familiar. Come now,
I'll tell myself, it isn't the first time,
you've seen them come and go.
The sun, of course, will be indifferent to my words.
Blood red, it will go down behind the far mountains
as if I were bereft in the world. There is no other sun.
The creator puts aside his handiwork,
the angels' verdict is in the locked book.

The gate must be closed, logic tells me. At night
the dark is darkest.

The man dressed in white
walked with sureness
in the night

And I followed him with hard eyes
step by step
as he passed by

And I understood that for me
there is no whiteness
in the night

And no light that can erase
even the farthest
of my griefs

But also there is no single
light
that can close the gate
a man in white opens in the night

The quiet light of flies
sinks. The desert answers
with a faint drum of hooves.

Silk scarves
sway from the spines of cactus,
and in the silvery tents
they are dancing the Dance of Jars.

Springs well up,
springs with their white stones,
springs with their musty deaths—
one bucket,
another,
and another,
they shiver in the wind like hanged men

and still there's time to rest,
the night drifts.

And still I've not said everything
I still have more to say

before the hour grows late and the crowd scatters
and each remembers then

what a man remembers when others are done
saying what they said and what they haven't said

and still I've not said everything

III

from ALL THE MILK
AND THE HONEY: 1966

III

Such joy, such pain, these are only words.
Conceal your joy. Gather your pain
into a safe place. Write only when your hand
needs nothing, not even the loose change
of the world. That which is crooked
cannot be made straight.
Don't go on repairing it.

Such joy, such pain, people say.
They mean something other: themselves.
Lie in wait; surprise yourself
in secrecy, in blood: when such joy appears,
such pain, tell yourself that a man
is not suited for such joy,
such pain forever, has no right
to strut it out on stage, no right
with such joy, such pain
to wound himself,
more, to wound others. Such joy,
such pain—didn't you know?—
they come and go.

The courage to wait
is greater than the courage to confess.
With pain it's easier to gain the sympathy
of others, which is not the case
with waiting.

You are alone here. You hang a picture
on the wall, straighten the rug, listen to footsteps pass,
think that you're miserable but remind yourself
in this you are not unique. Yet carefully
you tear a letter into shreds.
Here you are wholly on your own: judge yourself,
if you must. But remember: this also
is not what matters.

And perhaps only music. Since the emotion
is obscure, call it what you wish.
Only music, perhaps. Here it is
of an evening, hesitant
in the absence of strong feeling,
uncertain. So David, in his day,
must have played. But Saul didn't suspect.
Manly and confident he hurled his spear
as if in David's song there stood forth
matters final and clear-cut
like the severed head of Goliath.

Sometimes late at night
I sit at the piano and play. What does one need?
How little one needs, to be sustained,

even here, not to speak of better worlds
in the future. Indeed,
how little. My skilled hands glide across the keys

and I play. Ah, if only I could play! Yet even this
is enough. I'm not like Saul with his envy.
How little one needs: the nightly calm descends, and

one almost can believe life is redeemed, that it's possible
to live even here, this spring, without
the whole cast of Genesis: God,

tree, apple, Eve, the serpent.

THIS SLOW UNEARTHLY SPELL

for Peter and Shulamit

This slow, unearthly spell of standing still.
Not to trade places with, or envy
those flying overhead at night, passing
in a shriek of polished and cold metal,
jostling each other in a mysterious light.

Not to set out again and again. To spend each evening
among familiar tokens, making
a barren speech before the stars. Keeping close watch
over time's steps. To bring to an end
all that is loved and rare
with an unhurried hand and a shattered heart.

1

I could cross the border
but I don't want to.

Besides, the evenings now
are cool and blue.

If I buy me
an elegant blue suit
and wear it into the street
I might stand out.

But I'll feel odd.

2

The birds are distant now
and twitter in other trees.
In the air, hints of September.

I'd like to travel
if only I knew where.

I'd like to find me a woman with a plait
who'll be content with this closet,
and if she isn't—
I'll buy us a large and spacious flat.
Four rooms.

3
A friend returns
from a long journey.
I look into his eyes.

There's no denying
something clings to him—
salt water or the sparkle of diamonds.

He speaks and I see
his pupils dilating:
The world is wide, life sweet.

I ask him what are his plans now.
What a question! He'll buy a hammer
and make the crooked straight.

My tailor is against parting.
That's why, he
said, he's not going away;
he doesn't want to part
from his only daughter. He's definitely
against parting.

Once, he parted from his wife
and he never did see her
after this (Auschwitz).
Parted
from his three sisters and
these he never again
looked upon (Buchenwald).
He once parted from his mother (his father
died at a ripe old age). Now
he's against parting.

In Berlin he was
my father's close companion. They passed
a good time in
that Berlin. The time passed. Now
he'll never go away. He's
most definitely
(my father died meanwhile)
against parting.

Orpheus walks this evening
in the footprints of Eurydice (the path is strewn

with pine needles). My lady, I am
leaving. My lady, I do not turn

my head to see the view,
neither to look at you. Lady,

do not be angry. I have with me
my violin, I can play to shorten

the journey. Approximately
at the third turn, hell became too beautiful:

red birds were blowing like sparks
in the burnt trees, early flowers

of an early blossoming. The vision of Eurydice's
soft nape. Always her nape. Oh, here comes

the spring! says the poet Orpheus
in his blundering heart:

To look back once, just
once. —The hand,

of its own volition,
is already arching over the violin.

Be attentive to this trembling shade.
Stretch out your hand to feel the wind, touch
carefully this tree. It's green, and greener still
at the crown, the trunk
a little bitten, though it still drinks deeply
from the earth which no one sees
in the city.
Be attentive, feel, touch carefully. Breathe in
the light, harder. Illuminate
each cloud. It's passing. And night
won't wait.

The apprentice in the shop across from me
—blacksmith or carpenter—
had a girl.
Each day at the close of work
(I end my work at eight,
then take a long or short walk)
I'd see her sitting on a stool
in her woolen cap, swinging her leg
to some recent tune
while the boy finished-up his work,

an hour late, as usual.
Now the girl is gone, and I don't know
who or what takes place at the blacksmith's
or carpenter's shop. But I know this:
winter passed and spring nights ooze like honey
from the lamp. And one must find, without delay,
rest equal to each pain, grief
in measure for the lover,
peace ample enough for those who sit late
keeping the hour.

And for this, time is brief,
the task is great.

It's not true, I tell myself;
it doesn't have to be so. It can be otherwise.
There were also other nights, kept safe
in memory.

So forget what frightened you, just now, in bed
and made you get up and light the lamp:
3 a.m. The woman of pearls and coal-black hair
is no farther tonight
than on all other nights.
She is almost here.

In this deep, clumsy darkness
remember me who stood before you
thirty-two years, to the day,
in this deep, clumsy darkness.

Remember me when you climb the watchtower
at dusk in a red spray of light.
Remember me when you drive away stray clouds
from this world to another

where clouds are forgotten.
Remember me among your flocks
more than you have remembered your other orphans
in this deep, clumsy darkness

where I am lost more than an orphan,
more than a lamb, for my eyes
are open, I can see how blue darkens, I am not
deceived: I see how blood thickens,

the voice stumbles, how everything returns
at evening to remind us and to speak for all
that has ever been, all that is changeless, homeless
in this deep, clumsy darkness.

A peaceful song. On such an evening, God, as this,
that falls like a truce, if I could sometimes sing
also a peaceful song, implore you
to turn the light of your face unto all
your worms, crawling wherever they are, loved
and unloved, appeased
and unappeased, God
and unGod.

IV

from NORTH-EASTERLY: 1979

VI

1

The problem, of course, is to shape a form
like a diamond, but also like an ample bed
where a man can stretch without
knocking his head against a wall,
and like a taut string
with no corners to catch dust.

2

What you are meant to say
you say with suspicious fluency.
What you wish to say
sometimes is said between the lines.
But what you make an effort to say
is not said, as if it were so meant.

3

And once again the evening sky—vast emptiness
in which clouds, planes are scribbling tiny streaks and curls.
They are the dynamic element: what is written and then erased.
And autumn confuses in you the ripe, plaintive fruit
that asks only to stop, to delay, to fix
each brilliance in the opening of the black gullet.
And this is impossible. For this there is no time.

4
The poet's time is always
too long or too short, like shoes
that pinch or slip.
What you wish to say to future generations
must be said now, but you keep busy
rummaging through drawers.
Perhaps it's better this way: last year's rain
no one but you remembers,
and words to your grandchildren
will not return to be revised and weighed.
Here, cunning is required. This is the static element:
to speak to the moment, like a journalist,
and hope it will stretch a little
or as much as possible.

A day of unplanned sunlight. A sea gull flares
above the roof, an open parachute.
Here is the sudden turn I too
should have been able to make.
At my age it's difficult.
But I tell myself: I'll try.
Without strain, however. The secret of beauty lies
in the effortless. A graceful thing
doesn't beat its wings—it sails,
floats, hovers
beyond the reach of antennas, iron combs
digging out bits of cant from the air.
A stranger won't understand how hard
it is for the ordinary newspaper reader
or the man standing in line to unfurl
his wings,
let alone do a proper job of anything.
To flap one's mouth, now and then,
is something else
entirely.

A starry night at last Van Gogh
in the café unabashed
whirling about like the moon in orbit
like stars
skimming the newspaper lit-up in mirrors drinking
not that I haven't heard
the sound of running water
but I said to myself the tap
there were impediments
there were extenuating circumstances
I am not a prophet nor the son of one
I was even wearing the slippers I carry with me
ready for nightmares such as this
on a wild night, a sleepless night.
How many canvases were abandoned and all
that was driven away returns as if summoned:
on a sidewalk at a local café
a man sits and hears his name—
Yes, I am aware. Yes, I recollect.
At last an unequivocal answer.
A starry night?
No. Not yet.

Everything begins with the morning shave,
ends with lights out at one or two.
Thus the daily order
can become a terrible disorder in the dark.

Not younger and not much older.
No need to complain yet, considering the years.
The beard is short and non-prophetic,
the glance exact and almost clinical
(the doctor trembling in the mirror is me).

The body doesn't hurt yet, but it's already a burden.
The belly sags, you learn to live with it.
The forces that once leapt free from the cage
return to it as destructive forces.

Thus and forthwith and so on and hence—
What's new? Nothing under the sun.
And whoever looks to a bad end
has not learned from bitter experience.

is a complicated business. Only one bird is an expert,
and even it, apparently, is never seen.
The first condition, of course, is ash: embers,
dead ashes, the ash of cigarettes,
almost anything. In the absence of ash,
broken-ends will do, plaster debris, a total collapse,
ruins. Whatever is anti-biological, anti-ecological.
A further condition is the ability to rise
and stand on your feet after the fall,
a condition found also in the boxing ring:
the odds are against you, you're in the late rounds,
even your fans have turned away, thinking
of home and supper.
When younger, I knew a man—an expert, certainly!—who rose
each Monday from the weekend's ashes
and each Friday from the week's ashes. Only a handful
of men are like this: a sort of resurrection artist
parallel to Kafka's hunger artist.
But for everyone who rose I met a number who didn't.
Some burned in a small fire, ordinary,
like the flame of a kerosene stove;
and some went up in a sudden blaze, like dry thorns,
accompanied by sirens and bells.
And in this men are no different than women,
the young no different than the old,
each person has his appointed hour.
And one occupation is like another—workers blaze up!
Exactly like clerks and those in the liberal professions,
despite the rumor they're more fireproof.
Only a few of these will rise again
and stand. One needn't despair at this. On the contrary,
your common birdwatcher will swear to it: the phoenix
is not a mythological creature. It's here among us,
but it's rare.

ANOTHER CITY

for Amnon and Daniella

Graham Greene in his elegant style:
"My roots are in the absence of roots."
Later, a style better suited for a tiresome task—
even in a train to Istanbul
it's possible to grow sick of writing,
more so in South America.
A man flies his typewriter
to five continents like someone
stepping out to relieve his dog
or spite the neighbors.

Squares of light in the plane window.
A seatbelt—to make certain nothing will burst forward
and the unexpected happen.
We have the freedom of choice,
but our choice is so limited:
a meat or vegetarian menu.

At the hotel the grave-faced concierge:
The first shall be the last . . . something like that.
But the suitcase grows lighter
after the tip.
And so, looking back, you see it was all worthwhile—
you could be born, God forbid! a politician
or not be born at all.

There remains then the worries of making a living.
A man needs a smile, a good word and a loan.
The rest needn't be mentioned.
The words photograph a given situation:
A body leaning against the headboard, glancing around the room,
—Not bad,
another city that tells it nothing.

Closing your eyes won't help. Who can condemn
the perfectly cunning bomb, the mine placed just so,
without some slight hope for change—like pointing
to an abscess or like a doctor
writing another dose for the dying.

Leave the world in men's hands and watch
what happens: a mob of predators
tearing at other predators—some small—
in butcher shops and on highways,
in bedrooms and voting booths.

Leave a city in the hands of architects,
contractors, city council:
yesterday, skyscrapers to plumb
the heavens. Today, hives
and cattle pens, holes stuffed with mortgages and loans,
squares circled dizzily by traffic.

And yet, always, there is this city:
you arrive near evening,
always on time, as scheduled,
happy with the white sheets on the bed,
and open the suitcase
and remove a book and glasses
and turn on the radio and forgive
whoever hung the mirror and the reproductions
and arrange a few notes for a talk
and remember a face or a photograph
and walk downstairs to survey the hotel bar
when the window fills with darkness
and tiny lights begin blossoming
in a city that's foreign and lovely
and yes, night falls
and it's yours.

As years go by,
the original plan is disrupted.

What was carved in stone keeps being erased
as if line and relief returned to the bosom of stone.

Marble becomes water-stained, the color of brick
is damaged, everything drips or washes away.

A shoe sinks in the canal
where only branches float.

The wooden stars on the lintel stream away,
the house-frame leans like a tree over water.

What was once cut in acute angles
rounds itself again and curls—like ripple

and net in the current, waves moving
with wind, waves folding over waves

when a boat passes. What is built on the sea
longs to be sea again. A window

throws its momentary patch of colored dye
into the water. It's dangerous to open a window.

There is no stone without its hour; there is no hour
that didn't carve in stone as a sediment
growing like marsh grass and seaweed.

TWILIGHT

Twilight, so as to be ready, practises
with a line and a steady hand—like a tattoo—

engraving the fixed times for loss;
the evening is honed to a skin

until it's fine, until it's sensitized, as if its end
is to be a film of glass transparent to its pain.

To be a stone is the dream of everyone,
but in their dream everyone carries a stone

and water covers the dream
and light wraps the face of the water

with a slack hard hand, hard slack
as if it made everything equal for now.

Amsterdam, December 1967

In night's realm the red hood
was torn from her head—
monster ancient as night
blind in the scalding mirror.

The tree at the window sill
whispers to itself.
The veteran wolf is haggling:
Grandmother or girl?

Up in the thick sky floats
a red hood.
Red blood at its feet,
blood of a slaughtered wolf.

Fog over the morning's face.
Particles of fog turn into particles of light—
light equally sown, gathered
into the sun's pale circle,

as if it renewed the green of an invisible meadow
which will then shine forth
deeper green, dripping with water.
This is the face of a land
that bears over and over again—

so much, it becomes alien.
Who'd dare recall a desert here?
In the prayer book in church even the desert
seems green, nestled in shadow.
It's easy to identify with your own,
and to you was given a wilderness unsown

and a light consumed
by promises and dreams: kine
and ears of corn and sheaves.
In the meantime
seven lean years, and after them
seven more, lest you forget. And in a short while
the cycle will be complete.
Thus time moves on, it destroys.

Here, time barely moves. In this fog
that tells you nothing of warmth
or tenderness or grief, among signs
that have never touched you,
apparently you grow. But a stranger's hand
gathered the harvest. What remains

Fog

is the memory of a broken mirror, an inward
habit, and a little green that enters
your eyes, in spite of itself—here and there,
blossoming.

Colchester, 1968

A young man leans from the window to gape
at the twilight, his body half-way out
in a redundant gesture.

A light breeze trembles the views of the water.
An impressionistic man in anxious gray
breaks off, for his private needs, a crooked piece

of the evening as a sign for pain.
A woman who wanted to enter the picture
hesitates at the edge of the still life.

The man has not yet finished his work.
The woman is not his wife.

There are no more details.

First day, month of June. Like a ship's captain
I make an entry: the river quiet, no fish, no fisherman.

Not a breath of wind, each leaf
hangs motionless, the mottled foliage

freezes in place—far shades graying a little,
near ones showing green.

"A bird is shot into the sky."
It's only twilight. This also is not freedom.

The wind brings peace to what was. To what never was,
wind does not bring peace. To one's surprise, this too
is a place: the poet brings it forth
with the breath of his mouth,
the writing of his eyes—an old ruse.
When I say *you*, already you smile. When I glance at my watch
you grow unhappy. Pretty girl, how little
you require, and what little profit there is in love.
This place is worse than hell:
Hell is, is real.

The boat rocked in the waves
its gunwale knocking against the pier
a firefly melted small points of fire
in the water
somewhere a dark metallic glint
of fish streaming in the undercurrents
beside a tree that lowered
its tide of branches to the water
marking an ephemeral fact we sat
and spoke easily of things
plain matters and matters that circled about themselves
a world adequate to itself and to me
you leaned your head back against your purse
you were telling the family tale
are you cold?
peals of laughter from the inn
at night laughter seems strained and unreal
a pretty profile
intense
a pale hunter turning gray

I pored and pored over the text to find
where she entered and who had a hand in it.
An amateur detective, I found
only footprints.

At the beach two bodies
joined on the sand, abandoned car,
typewriter—enough for a typical
lethal plot. The radio playing.

Once it was risky.
Nude photos in the drawer.
A small box, empty and yellowing.
A pair of nylons. In September or December.
I'm writing this down from memory.
Up to this point everything is clear.

Having no way out, words join
in a small, compulsive rhythm. The foot taps it.
The ritual varies from country to country
but keeps its own logic:
once every year.

Alone, slowly, the knife blade dances,
works the abstractions, strips away,
veil after veil falls: I'm not
the first. I slept
beside her almost a year.
So what.

As the years pass, the magus grows withdrawn and weak;
the rare that was a daily presence
dwindles into an unexpected guest.
The rest of the time you read the world
in the news and the palm of your hand.

What was taken for granted became
a kind of revelation.
The constant search, so little to be desired,
became itself the end:
half the sky is in the light of a dying day,
half threatening a storm—

once more a sign is given of days
burning anew in our riddled flesh,
the miracle restored.
Thus towns and countries go rushing by

in the train window, an unreliable
interpreter. But you stop
in the twilight of a winter's evening, here
in this darkening city, before sleep,
to witness again the secret.

Summer, and a land stirring—a gust of warm wind
and camels in the street, a swarm of bees
lifting in smoke. The remnant of the Canaanites
is spilling into the streets.

These are the waters that wear down the stones
and deepen the hidden cleft of the well. In the Book,
Rachel still goes down with her jar, the moon rises
and gnaws holes in the darkness.

The old frenzy in the blood
still stones the living. And a harsh hand
soothes the forehead with a damp rag,
promising the sick man in his bed

that truly his night shall be sweet.
There is something in promises—
remote, a secret wrapped in desires
no one can unravel—

the wadi winding its way,
the city that rose from salt,
the strange end of Job:
forms of things to come.

In familiar landscapes
I get lost in what is unclear to me.
The linen wick dipped in oil
refuses to burn.
Not that I suddenly grew weary,
but the old familiar fatigue keeps
nailing me to rocks and salt.
When evening comes, once again
the armies of the uprooted
march in my blood.
Even though I kept so distant,
more than Vogel* perhaps,
there's something despotic
in this closeness:
that I managed to slip away,
I almost picture myself as a victim.

*David Vogel (1891–1943): Hebrew poet, born in Podolia, wandered
through Eastern and Western Europe during World War I and II. He briefly
visited Palestine but returned to France where he was captured by the Nazis
and killed in a concentration camp.

The old man holding the oar,
the man in shadows, the miller,
the couple making love in the barn
confirm the distant rumor of life
spoken of in rumors.
Night after night they stand near us,
spirits captive of their past—
once they resembled us
and could, if they so desired, sing.
Look! A youthful evening is falling
and they all return, the old with the young.
Oh, there's never an end to sorrow,
but also there is no sorrow in the world.
Frozen like figures of wax
far from the honey we gathered,
they turn our lives as well,
in their own way, to honey.
So open your window to the evening
and let the wind-shapes enter—
the old man holding the oar,
the man in shadows, the miller,
the couple crying out in the night—
to testify that nothing is lost here
and that nothing is here but what is lost
and that all their wants are laid upon us
and that they rest in peace at last.

The countries we live in
are ambiguous
and extend in different directions,
far off into the vistas
beneath the balcony.
These flickering lights
are also typical lights—
landscapes, elements,
their end: to go on. Their end: to go out.
The sun also rises and the sun goes down
following its path to the sea
through the narrow corridor set aside for it.
From east to the uttermost end of west
there is no new shadow
and the order of things is good—
also, there is no other order.
Here is tranquillity and peace at day's end
for a tired body and a spirit
sick of itself, rebellious—
this also is true. And a bird
filling with blood
is a falling bird, a rising bird,
better than these, a small bird in the hand
—Look! how soft its down,
a blackbird, its color lovely to behold.
And the other two have flown.

Peter Everwine is the author of *Collecting the Animals* and *Keeping the Night*. He has previously translated a collection of Nahuatl poems, *In The House Of Light*.

Shulamit Yasny-Starkman, a native Israeli, has translated widely from the work of Hebrew poets. She is currently at work on the poems of David Vogel.